Desserts
and other festive food

Dr Clemency Mitchell

Contents

First published in 2010
© 2010 Autumn House (Europe) Ltd
British Library Cataloguing in Publication Data. A
catalogue record for this book is available from the
British Library.
ISBN 978-1-906381-88-2
Published by Autumn House Ltd, Grantham,
Lincolnshire.
Designed by Lydia Hamblin
Printed in Thailand.

Part 1

Desserts

and other sweet things

Tarts, pies and cheesecakes

Wholemeal pastry

1 cup whole-wheat flour
1 cup rolled oats
½ cup water*
⅓ cup oil

*To make a sweet pastry, substitute apple juice concentrate or honey for some of the water.

- Mix ingredients together and roll out.
- As whole-wheat pastry breaks up rather easily, roll it out on a piece of cling-film or greaseproof paper, which will make it easy to transfer to the pie dish.
- For a pre-cooked pie shell, roll out pastry thinly, line pie dish, pricking the base with a fork. To ensure that the empty pie shell keeps its shape in the oven, fill it with dried beans. Bake it for 15-20 minutes in a moderately hot oven.
- This amount of pastry makes two pie shells, or one covered pie, using a 9 inch (23 cm) pie dish.

100% wholefood no oil sweet pastry

1½ cup porridge oats
1 cup whole-wheat flour
1 cup date butter (dates softened or blended
in just enough water to cover them)
1½ cups sunflower seeds, ground in blender
½-1 cup water

• Mix everything together and roll out, as in
previous recipe.

Crunchy granola base

• To make a supply of granola (homemade crunchy breakfast cereal) thoroughly mix together 4 cups porridge oats, ½ cup desiccated coconut, ½ cup sunflower seeds, ¾ cup nuts, ¼ cup oil, ¼ cup honey, malt extract or apple juice concentrate.
• Spread it on baking trays and bake in a cool oven, stirring occasionally until golden brown and dry.

Easiest crunchy base for a creamy pie or cheesecake: just spread granola in the bottom of the dish.

Standard granola base
• Briefly grind 2 cups granola or other crunchy cereal, mix with about 3 tbs water or orange juice and 1 tsp ground coriander.
• Press mixture over base of dish. This is suitable for an 8 x 10 inch (20 x 25 cm) dish.
• If the pie filling is not to be cooked and you want the base to be crunchy, bake until dry in moderate oven.

8

Apple pie

Wholemeal pastry – see pages 4 and 5.
Use a little more than half of the pastry for
the base.

Filling:
2-3 cooking apples
½-1 cup raisins

• Peel and slice the apples. Fill the pie shell
with alternate layers of raisins and sliced
apples. Cover with the rest of the pastry,
making a small central hole to let the steam
out. Brush the top with soya milk.
• Instead of raisins, you can sweeten with
¼-½ cup apple juice concentrate.
• Bake in a moderately hot oven until the top
is golden brown.

French apple tart

1 uncooked pastry base
Whole fruit jam or other fruit spread
Apple sauce (whole apples, cut in chunks,
cooked, blended and sieved)
2 or 3 cooking apples, cut in slices
Apple juice concentrate

- Spread the pastry base with jam or spread.
- Add a thin layer of apple sauce and arrange the apple slices on this, overlapping them, in a circular pattern.
- Lastly drizzle apple juice concentrate over the top.
- Cook in a moderately hot oven for at least half an hour. Cover with a piece of foil if the apples are browning too fast.

Lemon tart

Blend:
3 cups pineapple juice
½ cup orange juice
¼-$\frac{1}{3}$ cup lemon juice
$\frac{1}{3}$ cup cornflour
¼-½ cup honey or apple juice concentrate
2 tsp oil (optional)
Grated rind of 1 lemon

• Cook over medium heat, stirring until thick, then pour into baked pie shell or onto granola base and cool.

Pineapple cream pie

1 cup cashews
1½ cups pineapple juice
3 tbs lemon juice
1-2 cups tinned crushed pineapple
¼ cup cornflour

• Blend the cashews until smooth, in just enough juice to cover them, then blend in everything else except the crushed pineapple.
• Transfer to a saucepan and cook until it thickens, stirring all the time.
• Stir in the crushed pineapple and transfer to baked pie shell.

Fruit tart

• Spread a baked pie shell with whole fruit jam or other fruit spread, then cover with apricot halves, sliced peaches, raspberries or other fruit.
• Pour agar jelly mixture over and serve when cooled.

Agar jelly topping for fruit tarts and cheesecakes

1 cup red grape juice (or other sweet fruit juice)
1¼ tbs agar flakes

• Mix together and bring to the boil, stirring constantly.
• Allow to cool and thicken a little, then pour over fruit in tart, or spread on top of cheesecake.

Carob pie

2 cups hot water
1 cup raw cashews
1-2 cups dates (depending on how sweet
you like it) softened in 1-2 cups hot water
¼-$\frac{1}{3}$ cup carob powder
¼ cup cornflour
1-2 tsp vanilla
1 cup hot water

• Blend the cashews smooth in just enough of the hot water to cover them. Then add the rest of the water and the other ingredients and blend again.

• Transfer to a saucepan and cook, stirring constantly, until it thickens, then pour over granola base. Sprinkle with toasted flaked almonds or desiccated coconut.

• This is good as a pudding as well – just let it cool in a serving dish instead of a pie shell. It's particularly good served with sliced bananas.

Creamy tofu cheesecake

½ cup couscous soaked in 1 cup of boiling
water
½ cup cashews
2 cups orange juice
½ cup honey or apple juice concentrate
2 tbs cornflour
3 tbs lemon juice
1 tsp vanilla
250g packet of tofu

• Blend the cashews smooth in just enough of the orange juice to cover them.
• Then add the other ingredients and blend briefly. Transfer the mixture to a saucepan and cook, stirring continuously, until it thickens.
• Pour onto a granola base and allow to cool. Serve as it is, or with fruit or agar jelly topping (pages 15 or 22).
• This cheesecake can also be baked: pour the uncooked mixture onto the base, smooth the top and cook in a moderately hot oven until it is solid (but not firm).
• Allow to cool before adding topping.

Fruit topping for cheesecakes
• Cook together 1 cup apple juice concentrate and 1 tbs cornflour until it thickens.
• As it cools stir in 2-3 cups blackberries, raspberries or sliced strawberries.
• If more sweetening is needed, add a little honey or muscovado sugar.
• Spoon the topping onto the cheesecake just before serving.

20

Lemon cheesecake

If the filling is not sweet enough for your taste, reduce the lemon juice or increase the sweetening. It's quite small so use a 7 inch (18 cm) tin.

½ cup apple juice concentrate or honey
1½ tbs cornflour
¼ cup oil
1 medium-sized lemon – rind and juice
¼ cup soya mik
250g packet of tofu

• Blend first 5 ingredients together until very smooth, then add the tofu and blend again. The mixture should be a thick cream.
• Pour it onto a granola base, and bake in the oven until it is firm – about 20 minutes in a moderate oven.

Agar jelly topping – arrange thin lemon slices on cheesecake before pouring the topping over.

50 ml water
½ tbs agar flakes
4 tbs apple juice concentrate or honey or to taste
2 tsp lemon juice

• Bring ingredients to the boil in a small saucepan, then gently pour over cheesecake. Allow to cool before serving.

Puddings

Danish apple cake

This is not a cake but a delicious pudding,
made with layers of apple purée and crumb
mixture, and topped with 'cream'.

• Apple purée: this needs to be *thick*, so
cook roughly chopped unpeeled apples in
minimum water, (blend if necessary) and
sieve.
• There is no need to sweeten it if you use
sweet apples such as Cox's. With sour
cooking apples, sweeten to taste.

Crumb mixture A: 3 cups brown bread crumbs, 1 cup desiccated coconut or ground nuts, ½ cup apple juice concentrate or liquid honey.

Crumb mixture B: the same except for 1 cup chopped dates instead of apple juice concentrate or honey. Put the chopped dates in the blender with the chunks of bread when you make the breadcrumbs. Mix together well, spread on a baking tray and toast in a moderate oven until lightly browned. Arrange layers of apple purée and crumb mixture in a deep glass bowl, starting and finishing with a crumb layer. Top with 'cream'.

Tofu cream topping

½ cup cashews
½ 250g packet tofu
½ cup soya milk
1 tbs honey or apple juice concentrate
A few drops vanilla essence
1 tbs lemon juice

• Cook the cashews briefly in just enough of
the soya milk to cover them.
• Transfer to the blender and blend until
smooth. Add everything except the lemon
juice and blend briefly.
• Transfer to a bowl and *very gently fold* in
the lemon juice which will help to thicken the
cream, and it will thicken further as it stands.

Fruit crumble

Traditional fruit crumbles use quite a lot of sugar, but you can use dates, raisins, or apple juice concentrate to sweeten.

Here are some suggestions:
• Apple and raisin
• Rhubarb and date
• Plum and blackberry with raisins

NB: Some fruits, particularly some apples, take longer to cook than the topping does, so partly cook them before you add the crumble topping.

• When using dried fruit to sweeten, use one cup of dried fruit to 2-3 cups of fresh fruit, depending how sweet the fresh fruit is.
• Add one cup of water for each cup of dried fruit plus 1-2 cups extra – depending on the size of the crumble.
• Fill your baking dish ½-²/₃ full of fruit, spread the crumble over the top, and cook in a moderately hot oven until the crumble browns and the fruit is cooked.

Crumble topping A

1 cup whole-wheat flour
1 cup rolled oats
¼ cup oil
Enough apple juice concentrate or honey to give it a crumbly consistency when mixed together lightly.

Crumble topping B

1 cup porridge oats
1 cup whole-wheat flour
1 cup dates soaked in enough water to cover
1½ cups sunflower seeds, ground in blender

• Mix it together, adding extra water if necessary to make it crumbly.

29

Puddings

Waffles

Very good waffles can be made without milk or eggs. The ingredients can be varied, the one important principle being that the batter should be liquid enough to pour easily into the waffle iron, and thick enough to cook through before the outside gets too brown. Waffle batter thickens on standing, so if you have time, let the batter stand for an hour or more. Otherwise, just add water as needed as it thickens up.

Adding some oil or replacing some of the flour with ground sunflower seeds will make a crisper waffle. Waffles tend to go soggy as they stand, so if you are making them for a lot of people, make them a little in advance, and keep them crisp in the oven, or reheat them in the waffle iron just before serving. Waffles are good reheated for breakfast the next day.

What to eat with waffles

• You can use them like bread, and spread them with anything savoury or sweet that you would spread on bread.
• For a dessert, serve them with maple syrup, apple sauce, whole fruit jam, fruit spread, carob pie filling, sliced bananas, peanut butter topping.

Corn-oat waffles

3½ cups porridge oats
½ cup cornmeal
2 tbs oil
3½ cups water or milk

Optional additions for sweet waffles:

¼ cup dates or 2 tbs honey
Vanilla or maple flavouring

Additions for savoury waffles:

A small onion, roughly chopped
Your choice of herbs
Salt or herb salt to taste

• Blend everything together for about 30 seconds.
• Pour into oiled and heated waffle iron and cook.

34

Tahini-oat waffles

2 cups water or milk
2 cups porridge oats
2 tbs tahini
2 tbs whole-wheat, barley or other flour
Vanilla or maple flavouring
1-2 tbs honey or apple juice concentrate or
2-3 dates
Pinch of salt

• Let the batter stand and thicken, then add
extra liquid as needed. Bake as for corn-oat
waffles.
• Both recipes freeze well. The easiest way
to thaw them is in a toaster.

Carob peanut butter topping for waffles

• Cook together for 5 minutes ½ cup water + ¼-½ cup carob powder.
• Transfer to blender and blend until smooth with ¼-½ cup dates softened in an equal amount of water, ½ cup peanut butter and a few drops of vanilla flavouring.

Fruit salads and smoothies

Fruit salads

Here are a few suggestions for some different kinds of fruit salad.

• Different colours, flavours and textures make interesting fruit salads.
• Dried and fresh fruits can be used together, and nuts often make a good addition.

Date and apple

- Dice one dessert apple for each person.
- Add several chopped dates and walnuts for each apple. Serve at once, or pour a little orange or lemon juice over to keep apples from going brown.

Quick winter fruit salad

- Sliced crisp unpeeled eating apples, chopped peeled oranges, a tin of pineapple chunks and, for texture and flavour, a handful of raisins.

Quick summer fruit salad

• Slice strawberries, bananas, nectarines, peaches or apricots, and sprinkle with toasted flaked almonds.
• Eat fruit salads with soya cream, coconut milk, cashew cream, tofu cream topping (page 25), fruit cream or smoothie.

Fruit salads and smoothies

• Smoothies, lollies and 'ice cream'

Smoothies are very quick and easy to make, and very versatile. They can be liquid enough to drink through a straw or solid enough to eat with a spoon like soft ice cream. They can also be frozen as ice lollies, or an ice cream machine can transform them into sorbets or ice creams.

Fruit smoothie

• Use any fruit and any juice. There should be enough juice to enable the blender blades to turn easily. You can use fresh fruit (reasonably small pieces), softened dried fruits or cooked or frozen fruits. Frozen bananas are very good. If berries with small hard seeds are used, the smoothie should be sieved. If it needs to be sweetened, use dates, raisins, honey, apple juice concentrate. Just blend it all together until smooth.
• Some smoothie suggestions: frozen banana, orange juice, dried apricots; peaches and raspberries with apple juice; mango with orange juice.

Cream smoothie

Frozen bananas* cut in small chunks
'Cream' – this can be coconut milk, tofu,
soya milk, cashews (be sure to blend
them until smooth before adding other
ingredients).
Fruit – any sort; berries or blackcurrants
(strain out the seeds) are especially good in
cream smoothies.

* To freeze bananas, remove skins, put in
airtight bags or containers and freeze.

Fruit whips

• Add a packet of tofu to a fruit smoothie mix and you have a quick and easy pudding to eat with crunchy cookies, or with a fruit salad. The recipe is very flexible; the exact proportions don't matter as long as it tastes good. You can serve it in individual dishes topped with toasted almond flakes, chopped nuts, pieces of fruit, or even granola.

Easiest possible apricot tofu whip

1 cup dried apricots cooked in orange juice
1 250g packet of tofu
1-3 tbs honey or apple juice concentrate if desired

- Blend until smooth.

Cookies, biscuits and bars

These recipes are all very wholesome, containing nothing refined, so they are very nutritious and a good choice for children's lunch boxes. They are very easy to make. Proportions need not be exact, and the choice of ingredients is flexible, too.

Date and coconut cookies

1 cup chopped dried dates, soaked in just
enough water to cover them
1 cup sunflower seeds, ground in blender
1 cup desiccated coconut
1 cup rolled oats
½ tsp vanilla essence

• Mix all ingredients together well and form into small balls, adding a little water if necessary.
• Place the cookies on an oiled baking tray and press them flat with a fork.
• Bake in a moderate oven until they are golden brown, then cool them on a wire rack. Makes 15-20 cookies.

Variations:

• You can use any seed, nut, dried fruit or flour, and any fruit juice instead of water.

• If you like it extra sweet, add an extra ½ cup of dates, or add 1-2 tbs of apple juice concentrate, runny honey or malt extract. If this makes it too sticky, add a little more oats.

• You can use nuts instead or as well as the coconut or sunflower seeds. Grind nuts in the blender first, or chop them finely.

48

• Try chopped dried apricots and/or raisins instead of dates, plus liquid to bind it.
• Apple sauce or mashed banana are two possibilities.
• If you like it spicy, add a teaspoonful of coriander seeds and a cardamom pod to the sunflower seeds in the blender. No blender? The cookies will just be more crumbly and chewy, but some prefer them like that anyway.
• Bars: spread the mixture about 2 cm thick on an oiled tray, and cut into bars or squares when cooked.

Cookies, biscuits and bars

Thin crisp biscuits

The ingredients are the same as for the cookies.
• If you are using chopped dried dates, rather than softening them in water, grind them finely in the blender. This works best if you grind them with seeds or nuts.
• Add enough liquid to make a dough that you can roll out thinly, cut into circles or squares and bake in a moderate oven until crisp (10-15 minutes). Cool on a wire rack.

Apricot bars

Crumb crust

4 cups rolled oats
1 cup whole-wheat flour
1 cup desiccated coconut
½ cup honey
½ cup oil

• Mix thoroughly. Place one half of the mixture in an oiled 8 x 12 inch (20 x 30 cm) baking tin. Spread with filling. Cover with the rest of the crumb mixture, pressing it down lightly. Bake until light brown. Cut into bars when cool.

Apricot date filling

• Cook 3 cups dried apricots and 1 cup dates in enough water to cover them. When soft, blend coarsely.

Apricot orange filling

• Soak and cook 1 cup of apricots in orange juice, then blend coarsely. Hand held blenders are best for small amounts of thick material.

Peanut butter or tahini flapjack

1 cup peanut butter or tahini
½ cup liquid honey
4 cups rolled oats

• Mix together thoroughly, press onto a flat baking tray (8 inches or 20 cm square).
• Bake in a moderate oven until firm and golden brown.
• Cut into squares or bars while still hot. Cool on tray or wire rack.

Granola fruit bars

1 cup porridge oats
1 cup whole-wheat flour
1 cup sunflower seeds
1 cup desiccated coconut
1 cup fruit – raisins, chopped dried apricots
or dried cranberries
A cup olive oil
¼ cup water
¼ cup soft brown sugar, malt, honey or
apple juice concentrate. If you use sugar
add an extra ¼ cup water.

- Mix everything together thoroughly.
- If necessary, add a little extra water to make it stick together. Spread about ½ inch (1½ cm) deep in an oiled tray.
- Press down well and smooth the surface.
- Bake in a moderate oven until golden brown. Cut into bars while still hot, and allow to cool in tray.

Part 2

Savouries

for social occasions

Here are some ideas for savoury dishes for sharing. Add a salad and a light dessert to make a complete meal.

Pizza and pasta

Tomato sauce and cheese are basic so here they are:

Cashew pimento cheeze

A 'vege-cheeze' that's good in pizza and can also be used as a spread and even sliced.
You can toast it too.
Blend until smooth:

1 cup water
3/4 cup cashew nuts or sunflower seeds
2 tbs sesame seeds or tahini
2/3 cup porridge oats
3 tbs yeast flakes
1 small onion
1 level tsp herb salt
1 clove garlic
2 tbs lemon juice, or to taste
½ cup tinned or fresh pimentos (sweet peppers)
⅛ tsp dill seed (optional)

• Use it in lasagne, for pizza topping, or use it for 'cheeze' on toast.
• To make a spread, cook it until it thickens, stirring all the time.
• To make into a brick for slicing, mix 4 tbs agar flakes in 1½ cups water and boil until flakes are dissolved. Use the above recipe, but substitute the 1½ cups agar mixture for the 1 cup water. Blend until creamy then pour into a mould and chill.

Tomato sauce for pizza, lasagne and other pasta dishes

• Sauté 1½ cups chopped onions, 1 chopped green pepper and 4 crushed cloves of garlic in 2 tbs olive oil and 3 tbs water.
• Add 1½ cups tomato paste, 2 tsp basil, 1 tbs honey or brown sugar, 4 cups tinned tomatoes, ½ tsp oregano and salt to taste.
• Simmer for about an hour if you have the time, otherwise use it as soon as it's cooked through. Add more water as needed. It can be frozen for later use.

Pizza

- Use whole-wheat bread dough.
- You could also use a scone dough, a pastry dough, or just use slices of bread.
- Cover generously with tomato sauce and add your choice of topping.

Possible pizza toppings

• Crumble 1 cup of tofu evenly over the sauce.
• Drizzle one cup of pimento cheeze (page 58) over the top in a lattice pattern.
• Top with a generous amount of sliced olives and sliced mushrooms.
• Make a nice pattern with sliced onion, green pepper rings and fresh tomato slices.

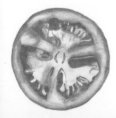

62

Other possibilities
• Sweetcorn, whole black olives, artichoke hearts, aubergine slices, sliced vegetarian sausage.
• Finish with a generous sprinkling of oregano or basil.
• Bake it at about 200°C for 20-30 minutes or until the dough is cooked.

Pita pizza

• Split pita in half and spread with pizza toppings. Bake in a fairly hot oven for 10-15 minutes.

Lasagne

• For a 9 x 12 pan, spread 1 cup of tomato sauce on the bottom. Cover with a layer of lasagne noodles. Cover with 1 cup tomato sauce.
• Crumble 1 cup tofu over the sauce, and dribble 1 cup pimento cheeze over tofu.
• Repeat the lasagne, tomato sauce, tofu and cheeze layers once or twice more.

- You can use TVP mince instead of tofu.
- Optional rich topping: use soya mayonnaise (page 72) as the final layer.
- Gratin topping: sprinkle fine brown breadcrumbs mixed with yeast flakes and oregano on the top.
- Bake for 45-50 minutes at 200°C. If the top is browning too fast, cover with foil.

Pasta al forno (pasta bake)

This is a very flexible dish. If possible use whole-wheat pasta and make your own tomato sauce. You can arrange it in layers, or mix it all together. Here are some suggestions for what to add: vegetarian sausage, cut in small slices, vegetarian mince, sliced or chopped mushrooms, lightly cooked diced or sliced vegetables, olives. Top with a layer of Cashew pimento cheeze (see page 58), soya (page 72) or tofu (page 70) mayonnaise.

For a super quick Pasta al forno with a creamy sauce:
• Blend ½-1 cup cashews until smooth in just enough water to cover.
• Add 1 medium orange or red sweet pepper cut in chunks, 1 onion in chunks, garlic cloves to taste, 2-3 tbs yeast flakes, herb salt to taste and 2 cups water. Blend.
• Mix with lightly cooked pasta and bake.

Useful toppings for baked pasta dishes

Creamy cashew sauce

3 cups water
½ cup cashews or sunflower seeds (or a mixture)
¼ cup cornflour, barley or other flour
1 onion, 1 clove of garlic, herb salt to taste

• Blend the cashews until smooth with just enough of the water to cover them.
• Add the rest of the ingredients and blend again. Cook gently for a few minutes, stirring until it thickens.
• Add more water for a thinner sauce.

Tofu mayonnaise (oil free)

1 250g pack of tofu
½ cup cashews, blended in just enough
water to cover
2-3 tbs lemon juice
1 tbs garlic purée
Herb salt to taste

• Crumble the tofu and add to the blender with the other ingredients and enough soya milk or water to enable the blender blades to turn easily.
• Blend together briefly. Option – add a handful of fresh parsley with the tofu and other ingredients.

Soya mayonnaise
(quite rich so use with care!)

1 cup soya milk
1 cup oil
2-3 tbs lemon juice
Seasoning – herb salt, garlic powder, etc.

• *Everything should be at room temperature.*
• Blend the oil and soya milk for about a
minute, add the seasonings, then *very gently
fold* (do *not* stir) in the lemon juice, which
will cause the mixture to thicken and it will
thicken further as it stands.

Couscous

This North African favourite is made from
wheat, and we recommend a whole-wheat
variety. It is quick and easy to cook. If there
are no instructions on the packet, place half
a cupful of dry couscous per person in a
bowl, add double the amount of boiling water
and let it stand for 1-2 minutes, until the
water is absorbed. Then put it in a steamer
over the stew (see page 74) and let it steam
for a few minutes. Transfer it to a large
but rather shallow dish and fluff it up with
a fork. Serve it at once by the plateful with
generous helpings of stew on the top.

Stew for couscous

• Make it in the lower half of your steamer.
You will need plenty of vegetables. Start
with a basis of onion, gently sautéed in
a little olive oil or oil and water, then add
chunks of carrot, swede, parsnip, celery or
celeriac, leek, courgette, aubergine, broccoli,
cabbage, whatever you like. Tomato purée
or tinned tomatoes are essential, and a tin of
chickpeas gives an authentic North African
touch. You can use TVP or other meat
analogues too.

74

• Add enough water to nearly cover the vegetables, and simmer gently until it is done.
• Flavour with vegetable stock cubes or seasoning salt, and add whatever other herbs or spices you like – garlic is strongly recommended, along with ground coriander, caraway and paprika.
• If you want it to cook quickly, cut the vegetables in small pieces, adding the ones that need to cook the longest first.

• If you want to save preparation time, chop them in big chunks, remembering they will take longer to cook. Excess liquid can be poured off and served separately.
• Problems with wheat? Use millet or quinoa instead of couscous – but remember it will take as long as the stew to cook. Leftover couscous reheats well, so make plenty.

Pilaf

This is a very easy dry rice dish, and an ideal way to use up leftover cooked rice. It is simply long grain rice mixed with a selection of colourful and tasty small items. It can be oil free, or the onions and other items can be sautéed in a little olive oil.

Rice for pilaf

2 cups long grain brown or white rice
5 cups water
Salt or vegetable stock cube to taste
Bay leaf
• For a golden pilaf, add ½-¾ tsp turmeric to the cooking water.
• For a very special golden pilaf add a pinch of saffron instead of turmeric to the cooking water.

• Put the rice, water and seasoning in a saucepan with a well fitting lid. Bring it quickly to the boil, then turn the heat right down and let it simmer until all the water is absorbed, about 45-50 minutes for brown rice, 20 for white. The grains should be soft and separate.

Suggested small items to add to rice:

Onion, celery, sweet pepper, green peas, carrot, courgette, mushrooms, olives, cashews, soya meat chunks, chick peas, sweetcorn kernels, artichoke hearts, chestnuts, vegetarian sausages – the larger items cut in fairly small pieces, and the vegetables lightly cooked or raw, according to taste.

• Add several cupfuls of items from the list and mix gently with the rice. The traditional way to serve it is in a large shallow dish and topped with a sprinkling of toasted flaked almonds and raisins.

Bobotie

A vegetarian version of a traditional South
African dish.
2 cups brown lentils, cooked
2 medium onions, chopped
2 cloves garlic, crushed
4 tbs olive oil
2 slices whole-wheat bread soaked in water
1 tbs smooth apricot jam or spread
1 tbs lemon juice
1 tbs fruit chutney*
1 tbs mild curry powder
1 tsp turmeric
Pinch of ginger
½ cup seedless raisins
¼ cup flaked almonds
Salt to taste
1½ cups of topping sauce**

• Sauté onions and garlic in oil. Add all the other ingredients, except for the sauce, and mix gently. Place mixture in baking dish and smooth the surface. Pour the sauce over the top and bake at 180°C for 45 minutes. Serve with yellow rice.

*Quick vinegar-free fruit chutney: Mix equal quantities of apricot all-fruit spread or jam and lemon juice.

**Creamy cashew sauce, white sauce, soya or tofu mayonnaise (see pages 68-72).

Yellow rice to serve with Bobotie

2 cups rice
1 cinnamon stick
1 tsp turmeric
1 tsp salt
5 cups water

• Combine ingredients and bring to the boil.
Lower heat and simmer gently till rice is soft
and water is absorbed. You can use either
brown or white rice for this recipe.

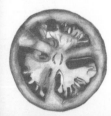

Haystacks

This is a favourite Mexican inspired meal. It has a variety of tastes and textures, and it's very easy to make.

It consists of a red bean stew, served on tortilla chips, with a variety of salads which can be piled on the top of the beans – like a haystack.

Red bean stew

1 small chopped onion
1 small chopped sweet pepper, red or green
1-2 crushed garlic cloves
1 tbs olive oil with 1 tbs water
1 tin red beans, drained
1 tin of chopped tomatoes

• Gently sauté the onion, pepper and garlic in the oil and water. Add the beans and tomatoes; seasonings such as cumin, sweet paprika and whatever other herbs or spices you like, and salt to taste.
• Add some vege meat or mince if you want to. Let it simmer while you assemble the other things. It should be quite thick.

Now arrange the rest of the haystack feast:

Tortilla chips – these are the one essential, and in addition serve any or all of the following:
Sliced olives, preferably the pimento stuffed kind
Tomatoes, chopped
Cucumber, sliced or diced
Onions thinly sliced or chopped
Lettuce, shredded
Mashed avocado or guacamole (see page 90), Cashew pimento cheeze sauce (see page 58), Vegan sour cream (page 89), or soya mayonnaise (page 72)

88

Vegan sour cream (oil-free sunflower or cashew creme dressing)

½ cup sunflower or cashew seeds, or a mixture
2 tbs lemon juice
½ tsp herb salt

• Add just enough water to cover the seeds and allow the blender blades to turn easily.
• Blend until smooth, then add lemon juice and salt. For a thinner cream, add extra water at the end.
• Option: add a clove of fresh garlic, ¼ tsp garlic powder or ½ tsp garlic purée before blending.

Guacamole

1 large ripe avocado
1 tbs lemon juice (or to taste)
1 small clove garlic, crushed
Salt to taste

- Mash everything together.

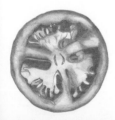

Part 3

Festive food

Here are a few ideas for festive food made from 100% unrefined plant foods. To really enjoy the meal, and leave room for dessert, serve modest portions to start with.

Festive food

Hot fruit punch

This makes 2 litres – 8 cups
1 tbs star anise
1 cup apple juice concentrate
1 tbs coriander seeds
1 cup orange juice
½ tbs whole cardamoms
1 lemon cut in thin slices
4 rosehip or other red teabags

- Simmer the spices in 1 cup of water for at least 10 minutes.
- Infuse the teabags in 2 cups boiling water for at least 4 minutes.
- Mix the spices, tea and juices, and add hot water to make up to 2 litres (1¾ pints).

A light salad starter:
Green, white and orange winter salad

Mix shredded Chinese leaf with watercress
or other dark green leaves with fresh orange
pieces, and serve with salt and a little olive
oil.

Festive nut roast

This festive nut roast is in three layers, with a lighter coloured layer in the centre, and prunes and apricots to make it extra special. Enough for 10-12 servings.

Basic dark nut roast mixture
for top and bottom layers

2 cups dark coloured nuts, such as walnuts
or walnut/peanut mixture
4 cups whole-wheat breadcrumbs
2 medium onions
2 sticks celery
1 cup water
2 tbs yeast extract (or more, to taste)
2 tbs mixed herbs

- Make the breadcrumbs and then grind the nuts in the blender.
- Next blend the onion, celery, yeast extract and water together.
- Now mix everything together and stir in the herbs. The mixture should be moist but firm. Add more water if it is too dry.

Middle light nut roast layer

Prepare in the same way, using
1 cup light coloured nuts, such as cashews
2 cups lighter coloured breadcrumbs
1 medium onion
1 stick celery
½ cup water
½ tsp herb salt, or to taste

- Thoroughly grease a loaf tin or deep ovenproof dish.
- Arrange the nut roast mixtures in 3 layers, with the cashew mix in the middle.
- Now take 9-12 ready-to-eat prunes and/or apricots, and stuff them one by one, evenly spaced, into the nut roast. Smooth over the top, and bake in a moderate oven for an hour, or until firm and starting to brown.
- Remove from tin or dish and place on a platter, surrounded with roasted cherry tomatoes and button mushrooms. Serve in slices, with relish, gravy and vegetables.

Nut roast en croûte (nut roast savoury roll)

This is nut roast mix encased in pastry. This can be wholemeal pastry (see page 4) or, for a special effect, bought flaky pastry, rolled out very thinly.

• Roll the pastry into a long rectangle.
• Make the nut roast mix into a long thick sausage shape and place it longways in the centre of the pastry rectangle.
• Bring the two edges of pastry together to enclose the nut roast.

- Turn it over, so the join is underneath and transfer to a baking tray.
- Brush the top with soya milk, and decorate with diagonal cuts or a criss-cross pattern.
- Bake in a moderately hot oven until the pastry is golden brown.

Non-nut savoury roll suggestions:

A savoury festive roll is really just a different shape of pie. Most things that can be put in pies can be used for savoury rolls. You can use any kind of bean, lentil or vegetable stew or roast, but it does need to be fairly dry. You can use porridge oats, rice flakes or breadcrumbs to absorb some of the fluid if it's too moist. Then make it according to the directions for Nut roast en croûte.

Nut-free alternatives

Sunflower and sesame roast

• Make as for nut roast, replacing nuts with a mixture of sunflower and sesame seeds.
• Grind the seeds briefly so a few are still whole.

Lentil roast

This can be turned out as a loaf, or just
spooned out of the ovenproof dish.
1 onion, whizzed in blender with 1 stick of
celery, a medium sized carrot and 1 cup
water
1 cupful red lentils
1 tin chopped tomatoes (2 cups)
½ cupful porridge oats
1 cup water
¼ tsp basil or oregano
1 tsp herb salt or other seasoning to taste
1-2 tbs olive oil (optional)

• Mix everything together, and put it into a
rather shallow ovenproof dish. Bake in a
moderately hot oven until it is firm – 1-1½
hours.

Vegetables for a festive meal

They have to be colourful, lightly steamed
and absolutely not soggy.
Suggestion: steamed sliced carrots with
broccoli florets and frozen peas.

Roast potato wedges

• Wash medium-sized potatoes and cut
them longways into 4-6 wedges. Steam
them until they are almost cooked, then
transfer them to a large bowl, containing just
enough olive oil to coat them lightly, your
choice of seasoning (see page 107) and salt
or herb salt.
• Mix, put them in a baking tray and cook
them in a moderately hot oven until they are
golden brown.

Seasoning variations:

• Red – add sweet Hungarian paprika
• Herb – add rosemary or other dried herbs
• Oil and lemon – use citronette salad sauce (one part of lemon juice to two parts of oil) instead of oil
• Fat-free version – use a little soya milk instead of oil

Roast parsnips

• Cut parsnips in wedges or chunks.
• Steam for a few minutes, then toss in a little olive oil and bake them in a moderately hot oven until they are crisp and golden on the outside.
• Be careful, as they cook much faster than potatoes.

Cranberry relish 1

1½ cups cranberries
1 cup chopped dates
1 cup orange juice
¼ cup mixed peel
¼ cup chopped walnuts

• Put everything into a saucepan, bring to
the boil and simmer until the cranberries are
cooked.

Cranberry relish 2

1½ cups cranberries
Apple juice concentrate, enough to just cover the cranberries
Grated rind of 1 orange
½ cup raisins

• Put everything into a saucepan, bring to the boil and simmer until the cranberries are cooked.

Other relish ideas

Apple sauce
· Wash apples, cut in chunks, cook, blend and sieve.

Apricot sauce
· Cook dried apricots in orange juice, then blend briefly – make it rather chunky, and add some lemon juice for an extra tang.

**Country Style gravy
Rich cashew version**

2 cups water
½ cup cashew pieces
1 tbs onion powder or ½ small onion
1 tsp garlic powder or 1 clove garlic
3 tbs soy sauce or 1 tbs yeast extract
1 tbs cornflour

• Blend the cashew pieces, onion and garlic in just enough of the water to cover them.
• When it's smooth add the other ingredients, including the rest of the water, and blend briefly.
• Transfer to a saucepan, and cook, stirring constantly, until it thickens, adding more water if desired.

Nut-free version

3 cups water
3 tbs whole-wheat flour and 1 tbs cornflour
1 tbs onion powder or ½ small onion
1 tsp garlic powder or 1 clove garlic
2 tbs soy sauce or 1 tbs yeast extract

• Blend everything thoroughly.
• Transfer to a saucepan, and cook, stirring
constantly, until it thickens, and then for a
further few minutes.
• Add more water for a thinner gravy.

Sweets for festive meals

Christmas mince tart

1 wholemeal pastry pie shell (10 in/25 cm)
1½ cups mincemeat
1 orange cut in thin slices
Honey or apple juice concentrate

- Spread a thick layer of mincemeat (page 117) on the pie shell.
- Cover the mincemeat layer with thin slices of fresh oranges, and drizzle honey or apple juice concentrate over them.
- Bake until the pastry is cooked, or if you use a pre-cooked pie shell, just bake until everything is thoroughly heated through.
- Serve warm with soya or other creme.

Mincemeat

The original mincemeat was made with
meat, fruit and spices. The meat was
omitted long ago, though some brands
are still made with suet. Most commercial
mincemeat is vegetarian now, but even the
health food store varieties tend to be very
sweet. Below is an all fruit recipe from an old
Scottish cookbook, which is quick and easy
to make.

All fruit mincemeat

1 cup raisins
1 cup currants
½ cup mixed peel
1 cup chopped grapes
1 cup chopped apple
½ to 1 tsp mixed spice*
Grated lemon rind and juice

• Add 1 cup water and cook together until apples and grapes are soft. It can be used as it is, or it can be minced or briefly blended first. If you prefer it sweeter, add apple juice concentrate to taste.

*Try coriander, cardamom and star anise for a different and delicious taste.
• Grind together 1 tbs star anise, 1 tbs coriander seed and ½ tbs cardamom pods. Keep it in a jar and use as you would mixed spice.

118

Moroccan date and almond truffles

1½ cups toasted almonds
1 cup chopped dates
1 tbs orange flower water
1 tbs honey
½ tsp cinnamon
½ cup shredded coconut

• Grind the dates and almonds together in the blender.
• Remove from the blender and mix in the next three ingredients. You may need to add extra liquid if the dates are very dry.
• Form into small balls and roll in the shredded coconut.

Fruit squares

1 cup raisins
1 cup dried apricots
1 cup dates
½ cup nuts
2 tbs lemon juice
2 tbs honey
Rice paper

- Mince the fruit and nuts in a food processor or mincer.
- Add the lemon juice and honey and mix well. It should be a very stiff paste.
- Spread it thickly (¾ in/2 cm) on rice paper. Smooth it with a rolling pin and cover it with another piece of rice paper.
- Place weight on top for several hours or overnight, then cut into squares or bars.

Dried fruit treats

These are expensive to buy but inexpensive and easy to make.
• Remove the stones from Deglet Nur or similar dates, and stuff with Brazil nuts, walnuts or almonds and marzipan.
• Do the same with soft and sticky ready-to-eat apricots.

Marzipan

• Mix ground almonds with enough honey to make a stiff paste and roll out and cut up as needed.

A few healthy ideas for children's parties

Parties are easy when all the children come from families with the same eating habits, but the low-sugar or sugar-free whole-food diet can seem very unattractive to children who are not used to it. The principle is to provide reasonably healthy food for the guests to *enjoy*, rather than to stick rigidly to the most natural and whole-food menu.

Children's parties

The food should be attractive to look at and enjoyable to eat, but not necessarily only the types of things you would want to eat every day. If you make a feature of the most beautiful, colourful and attractive natural plant foods, you can give yourself a little leeway in the other items on the menu. Here are some suggestions:

- **Fruits**: A large bowl of fresh strawberries or cherries in summer, a basket of clementines in winter; apples and pears in small sizes, bite-size chunks of pineapple on sticks, sprigs of three or four grapes.
- **Savouries:** Cherry tomatoes, raw vegetable strips (carrot, cucumber, pepper, etc.) with dips. Tortilla chips or potato crisps are very popular party foods, and why not, once in a while? Most children love sausages too, and even little meat eaters usually find vegetarian sausages very acceptable.

- **Sandwiches:** As some children may find the healthiest sort of whole-wheat bread unappealing, use a lighter bread and make tiny sandwiches with a variety of attractive fillings.

With all those good things on the menu, the usual cakes, jelly and ice cream can take a smaller place.

- **Ice cream:** There are several varieties of vegan ice cream available at health food stores and large supermarkets. If you want to avoid this sugar-rich vegan treat, make ice lollies or even ice cream using a fruit smoothie mix.

• **Jellies:** You can find vegan jellies in supermarkets too.
• **Biscuits:** 'Cookies' usually have the most wholesome ingredients whether bought or homemade.

Children's parties

- **Cakes:** Cakes are beyond the scope of this book, but there are vegan recipes for all sorts of delicious cakes in vegan cookbooks and websites, with varying degrees of natural ingredients, so take your pick.
- **Drinks**: Sparkling water, fruit juice such as apple or grape diluted with equal parts of sparkling water, cold rose hip tea generously sweetened with apple juice concentrate, fruit smoothie.